CONTENTS

FLOWER BEETLE

FLOWER BEETLE FACTS

SIZE: 4 mm to 11 cm long
HOME: worldwide except Antarctica
EATS: nectar, pollen, fruit

Check out this beetle's funny horn! This is a striped love beetle, but maybe 'Y-fronts beetle' would be a better name for it! It uses its horn to fight over females.

Flower beetles use their back wings for flying. Like all beetles, they have hardened front wings that act as protective wing cases.

WEIRD OR WHAT?

Male goliath beetles weigh about the same as a hamster!

Flower beetles include the giants of the insect world. The African goliath beetle can grow longer than 10 centimetres and it has bigger wings than a sparrow!

LEAF BEETLE

LEAF BEETLE FACTS

SIZE: around 12 mm long
HOME: worldwide, especially tropical areas
EATS: leaves

This handsome fellow is a leaf beetle. Leaf beetles are named after their favourite food – leaves.

With plants on the menu, it's no surprise that many leaf beetles are pests. Gardeners hate the scarlet lily beetle. It destroys their prize lilies.

WEIRD OR WHAT?

Lily beetle larvae cover themselves in their own powdery poo. It acts as sunscreen and puts off predators, too!

Colorado beetles and their larvae feed on the leaves of potato, tomato and aubergine plants. They breed so quickly – and feed so quickly – that they can wipe out a farmer's crop.

Tortoise beetles are a kind of leaf beetle. They feed on leaves and damage garden plants. This golden tortoise beetle likes morning glory leaves best.

WEIRD OR WHAT?

The golden tortoise beetle can change colour! Its body can look golden or red, like a ladybird's.

Tortoise Beetle

The tortoise beetle is named for the distinctive shape of its wing cases, which look like a tortoise's shell.

Female tortoise beetles make good mums. This one is looking after her eggs.

TORTOISE BEETLE FACTS

SIZE: 5 mm to 1.2 cm long
HOME: worldwide, especially tropical areas
EATS: leaves

Tortoise beetle larvae stick close to their brothers and sisters. Their bodies are usually spiky to put off birds and other predators.

TIGER BEETLE

The tiger beetle isn't striped, but like its big cat namesake it's a fierce and skilful predator. It runs down prey on its long legs.

WEIRD OR WHAT?

A tiger beetle can speed along at 9 kilometres per hour. Relative to its size, it's more than 20 times faster than an Olympic sprinter!

TIGER BEETLE FACTS

SIZE: 1-2 cm long
HOME: worldwide, especially tropical and subtropical areas
EATS: insects (eg ants), other minibeasts (spiders, worms), tadpoles

The tiger beetle uses its long jaws to seize its prey and tear it into pieces. Then it spits up some saliva to digest the prey before sucking it up.

Some tiger beetles live in trees, but most are ground dwellers. This tiger beetle is hunting among the leaf litter.

11

Imagine feeding your babies on dung! That's what dung beetles do.

SIZE: 5 mm to 2.5 cm long
HOME: worldwide except Antarctica
EATS: dung

DUNG BEETLE

Dung beetles collect animal dung and roll balls of it along the ground. The balls are bigger than they are.

WEIRD OR WHAT?

Anyone for tennis? The largest dung balls are as big as tennis balls.

Dung beetles lay their eggs in the dung balls. Their larvae feast on the dung when they hatch.

These duelling minibeasts are stag beetles. The males do battle to win or defend territory.

STAG BEETLE FACTS

SIZE: 8 mm to 10 cm long
HOME: woodlands, worldwide
EATS: tree sap, rotting fruit
       (larvae eat wood)

STAG BEETLE

Stag beetles fight each other with their super-large jaws, or mandibles. These look a bit like stags' antlers, which is how the beetles get their name.

WEIRD OR WHAT?

In some stag beetle species, the jaws make up half of the body length.

There are no prizes for guessing how the rhinoceros beetle got its name!

RHINOCEROS BEETLE

You might get a surprise if you disturb a rhino beetle. It hisses!

Rhinoceros beetles are a kind of stag beetle. The male has an impressive horn for digging and fighting. It uses its horn to push and shove its rival.

14

The hercules beetle is one of the largest rhino beetles. Its horn can be 10 centimetres long.

The hercules beetle is named after the strong hero in ancient Roman myths. It can carry 850 times its own body weight on its shell.

RHINOCEROS BEETLE FACTS

SIZE: 2.5 cm to 13 cm (excluding horn)
HOME: temperate and tropical forests
EATS: nectar, plant sap, fruit
(larvae eat wood)

Do you look like your mum and dad? Beetle babies don't. This is a hercules beetle larva. It spends a couple of years like this, then it makes a pupa and changes into its adult form.

WEEVIL

This beetle looks like it has an elephant's trunk! It's an acorn weevil, and uses its long snout to bore into acorns.

All weevils have super-long noses. Most are fussy eaters that feed on just one kind of plant. Some are pests. This red palm weevil damages date and coconut crops.

WEEVIL FACTS

SIZE: usually less than 6 mm long
HOME: worldwide except Antarctica
EATS: plants

Some weevils are real showstoppers. This one lives in the rainforests of Papua New Guinea.

Most weevils have plain colouring, so that predators don't notice them. These two must win the prize for the best camouflage.

WEIRD OR WHAT?

In North America, boll weevils are a cotton farmer's worst nightmare. Each year they chomp their way through nearly 5 million bales of cotton.

With its amazingly long neck, this weevil from Madagascar has to be the strangest of all. Its name? The giraffe weevil!

Firefly

Check out this glowing bottom! Despite its name, the firefly is a beetle, not a fly.

Fireflies have a neat trick – bioluminescence. This is the ability to make light with their bodies. Fireflies flash to let other fireflies know where they are.

FIREFLY FACTS

SIZE: 45 mm to 2.5 cm long
HOME: tropical and temperate areas
EATS: other larvae, snails, slugs, pollen, nectar

WEIRD OR WHAT?

One female firefly uses light as a trap. She mimics the flashes of a different firefly species. When males approach to mate with her, she gobbles them up!

Violin Beetle

With its wide wing cases and long, slim head, this beetle is shaped a bit like a violin.

The beetle's flat body allows it to live under tree bark or among bracket fungi. It uses its slender head to nose about for grubs.

WEIRD OR WHAT?

Don't fiddle with a violin beetle. If threatened, it sprays a chemical powerful enough to paralyze your fingers for 24 hours!

VIOLIN BEETLE FACTS

SIZE: 10 cm long
HOME: rainforests, Malaysia
EATS: insect larvae

JEWEL BEETLE

This gem from Australia is a jewel beetle. In some parts of the world, craftworkers use jewel beetle wings to decorate jewellery and clothing.

Jewel beetles come in a rainbow of colours. It's hard to say if this one's orange, yellow, blue or green. It's all these colours – and more! – depending on the light. This is called iridescence.

The biggest jewel beetle is the ceiba borer. Its larvae feed on the wood of kapok trees. Some Native Americans in Mexico eat ceiba borers. Roast beetle, anyone?

WEIRD OR WHAT?

One jewel beetle likes to lay its eggs in the trunks of burned trees. Called the black fire beetle, it can sense a forest fire from many kilometres away.

JEWEL BEETLE FACTS

SIZE: 3 mm to 10 cm long
HOME: tropical forests
EATS: wood

BOMBARDIER BEETLE

'Fire!' This bombardier beetle is spraying boiling-hot, poisonous liquid. It does this in self-defence.

BOMBARDIER BEETLE FACTS

SIZE: 2 mm to 3 cm long
HOME: North America, Africa, Asia
EATS: other insects

When the hot fluid comes into contact with the air, it explodes with a loud 'Pop!'. The sound combined with the spray will see off most predators.

BLISTER BEETLE

WEIRD OR WHAT?

Sometimes blister beetles get into horses' hay. If a horse eats enough of the beetles, it dies.

Ouch! Blister beetles produce a nasty chemical that makes your skin blister.

Bees should tell this blister beetle to 'Buzz off!' Its larvae trick bees into carrying them back to their nest – where they feast on bee eggs!

BLISTER BEETLE FACTS

SIZE: 3 mm to 2 cm long
HOME: worldwide except Antarctica
EATS: insects, flowers, leaves

23

LONGHORN BEETLE

These stripy feelers belong to a golden-bloomed grey longhorn beetle. That name's quite a mouthful, considering the beetle itself is only 2 centimetres long!

The longhorn beetle family is enormous. There are more than 20,000 different species.

This beetle feeds on wild flowers and lays its eggs in thistle stems.

LONGHORN BEETLE FACTS

SIZE: 3 mm to 16 cm long
HOME: temperate and tropical forests
EATS: wood

This longhorn is a great capricorn beetle. It lives in deciduous trees, especially oaks. It only lives for about a month in its adult form, but spends 3 to 5 years as a larva.

The harlequin beetle's patterned wing cases help it blend in with tree bark. The males don't just have long horns – their freaky front legs are longer than their bodies!

WEIRD OR WHAT?

Tiny minibeasts called pseudoscorpions sometimes hide under harlequin beetles' wings, hitching a free ride to new feeding or mating grounds.

Some longhorn beetles resemble dangerous insects to put off predators. This yellow-and-black one looks a bit like a wasp.

DIVING BEETLE

SIZE: around 3 cm long (adults)
HOME: fresh water
EATS: aquatic insects,
crustaceans, tadpoles

This beetle pair are underwater! They are diving beetles, and they live in freshwater streams, rivers and lakes.

WEIRD OR WHAT?

Great diving beetle larvae are twice as long as their parents!

Like their parents, diving beetle larvae are fierce predators. They hunt and eat tadpoles and other aquatic prey.

WHIRLIGIG BEETLE

If you look on the surface of a freshwater pond, you may see small groups of small, shiny beetles.

WEIRD OR WHAT?

Whirligig beetles have two-part eyes, so they can see above and below the surface of the water at the same time.

Whirligig beetles are named for their behaviour when they are threatened – they whirl round and round in circles.

Just like shoaling fish, whirligig beetles hang out in a group as a way of avoiding being eaten.

WHIRLIGIG BEETLE FACTS

SIZE: 3 mm to 3.5 cm long
HOME: fresh water
EATS: aquatic insects

BURYING BEETLE

Burying beetles are the funeral directors of the insect world. They sniff out decaying animal bodies and bury them. This beetle is about to land on a dead mouse.

BURYING BEETLE FACTS

SIZE: around 12 mm long
HOME: worldwide except Antarctica
EATS: rotting flesh, maggots, animal droppings, plant sap

Burying beetles work as a team to bury bodies much bigger than themselves. They scoop out the earth beneath a carcass so that it sinks below the soil.

Burying beetles sometimes murder their own babies! They do this if they've produced more young than their underground larder can feed.

The beetles lay their eggs inside the corpse. The larvae of these beetles will have their own private larder of rotting chipmunk meat!

Here's another flesh eater! This red-breasted carrion beetle belongs to the same family as burying beetles, but it doesn't bother to bury the corpses it finds.

GLOSSARY

aquatic Found in water.

bioluminescence The ability of a living thing to produce its own light.

camouflage Colours or patterns that help an animal to blend in to the surrounding environment to avoid being seen by predators, prey or both.

carrion The meat (flesh) of a dead animal.

crustacean An animal with two-parted legs and a segmented body covered by a hard outer skeleton (an exoskeleton). Crabs and shrimps are crustaceans.

deciduous Describes a plant that loses its leaves for part of each year.

digest Break down food in the body.

iridescence The property of appearing to change colour from different angles, according to the light.

larva (plural larvae) The young stage of an animal, usually an insect. The larva looks different to its adult form.

leaf litter The layer of rotting leaves on a forest floor.

nectar A sweet substance produced by flowers to encourage pollinating animals, such as insects.

paralyze To make something unable to move.

pollen A powder that contains a flower's male sex cells. When these join the female sex cells of another plant, that plant can produce seeds. Some plants rely on the wind to carry pollen to different plants; others depend on pollinating animals, especially insects.

predator An animal that hunts and kills other animals for food.

prey An animal that is hunted and killed by another animal for food.

pupa (plural pupae) The life stage in an insect's life when it changes from one stage to another, for example from a soft-bodied larva to an adult with a hard outer casing (exoskeleton). Pupae are inactive and have a protective coating.

rainforest A forest habitat where rain falls almost every day. In a tropical rainforest, the climate is hot and steamy all year round.

sap Sugary fluid produced inside the stem or trunk of a plant.

species One particular type of living thing. Members of the same species look similar and can reproduce together in the wild.

temperate Describes the two regions of the earth that lie between the tropics and the poles, where the climate is warm in summer and cold in winter.

territory The area that an animal defends against other animals, usually of the same species.

tropical Describes the warm part of the world near to the equator (the imaginary line that circles the middle of the earth).

wing case In beetles, one of the hardened front wings that protect the papery back wings.

30

FURTHER INFORMATION

Books

Amazing Insects: Images of Fascinating Creatures by Michael Chinery (Firefly Books, 2008)

DK Science: Buzz by Caroline Bingham, Ben Morgan and Matthew Robertson (Dorling Kindersley, 2007)

I Like Weird Animals: Bomb-Factory Beetles and Other Weird Insects by Carmen Bredeson (Enslow Elementary, 2009)

Stinkbugs, Stick Insects, and Stag Beetles by Sally Kneidel (John Wiley & Sons, 2000)

Weird Wildlife: Insects by Anna Claybourne (Belitha, 2002)

DVDs

David Attenborough's Life in the Undergrowth (2 Entertain Video, 2005)

Natural History: Insects and Arachnids (www.a2zcds, 2007)

Websites

BBC Wildlife Finder
www.bbc.co.uk/nature/order/Beetle

National Geographic: Dung Beetles
kids.nationalgeographic.com/kids/animals/
creaturefeature/dung-beetle/

Natural History Museum
www.nhm.ac.uk/nature-online/life/insects-
spiders/bug-forum/?q=image/tid/25

Pestworld for Kids: Beetles
www.pestworldforkids.org/beetles

INDEX